ACCEPT YOURSELF OR DIE

FROM MORMON MISSIONARY TO TRANS PUNK

IMOGEN REID

Accept Yourself or Die:
From Mormon Missionary to Trans Punk

Imogen Reid

Sheer Spite Press
www.sheerspitepress.ca

Editing, design, and layout by Lee Pepper for Sheer Spite Press.
Copy-editing by Kat Rogue.
Cover and inside cover art are collages by John Bingley Garland, used under public domain.

Library and Archives Canada
ISBN 978-1-7753304-1-7

After two fucking years: I'm home, I'm free, I'm alone.

Two years of rules and church and prayer and isolation from family, friends, the "opposite sex," music, movies, books, art. Two years cut off from my name, my identity, myself. I'm standing, at last, in the small basement bedroom I shared with my brother and cousin, both of whom are a year into their missions. The room is a time capsule from a lifetime ago. I climb into the top bunk without bothering to undress or get under the covers. I crash out instantly, still wearing my missionary outfit, ubiquitous name tag still clipped to the breast pocket of my white button-up shirt.

I had barely fallen asleep when my aunt burst into the room, her face a picture of panic: "There's been a mistake, they sent you home early. We've got to get you on the plane".

The terror grips me at the realization I have to go back. I frantically protest to no avail as my family rushes me out the door, my protests ignored, the fear increasing to an unbearable climax.

I awake in a panic, a shout of protest frozen in my throat. My eyes dart around the room, and relief washes over me. I'm home. It was just a nightmare.

For weeks after coming from serving a two-year mission for the Church of Jesus Christ of Latter-Day Saints, I would have this same nightmare: there was a mistake, and I had to go back.

If you were in a room full of people who had been on a mission and you asked them, if you had the opportunity to do a second mission, would you do it? Not a single one would say yes.

It's hard to know where to start, because it's hard to know what parts of your own life are weird or interesting.

When we lived in Timmins as kids, our house was really overcrowded, and my brother lived in an uninsulated shed out back. Later, as an adult, he mentioned this later to some of his friends at church, laughing about it, and one of them said, "That's really messed up."

So he called me and asked, "Did we have a messed-up childhood?" and I had to tell him, yeah, we definitely did.

door to door

Going door-to-door doing missionary work was the worst.

Most people don't want Mormons knocking on their door, so people were usually pretty pissed off. One of my friends had someone open the door and put a gun to his head.

Mormons believe that if you get killed on your mission, you automatically go to heaven. A lot of guys believe that and it goes to their head, thinking that they're God's special servants and God will protect them. My companions always tried to get me to go with them even if there was a mean pit bull in the front yard, but I really didn't think God was going to protect me from getting bitten by that dog. In fact he didn't, when I was bit by a pissed-off dog right on my ass as I was trying to scramble over a fucking white picket fence as Elder Cecil (as you can guess by the name, he was from the deepest of the deep south) was laughing and trying to calm the dog down.

Even apart from dog attacks, I also just had really bad social anxiety, and I'd be panicking the whole time.

What I was good at, though, was relating to people. My mission is where I learned to listen without judging, and take people as they are. I learned that people are people: some are good, some are bad, some are evil, but most of us are just a bit broken and want to be seen and heard while we try and get through life.

A lot of the other missionaries were home-schooled, and grew up in a bubble their whole lives, but I'd been around non-Mormons my whole life, and I wasn't really all that interested in pushing the church on people anyways.

For a lot of missionaries, people are just numbers. They're just trying to get as many people as possible to join the church, and they don't actually get to know anyone. You have to call your district leader every week and give them your numbers. And when you get home from your mission, people ask you, "how many people did you baptize?" My numbers were terrible, but I'm glad now that I didn't bring many people into this shit.

I like people, though, and I'm interested in people, and a lot of people could tell that I was just talking to them as a person and not really trying to convert them. Also, I swore a lot, 'cause I grew up around real people, and while it earned me the side-eye of many a pious missionary, it helped normal people trust me. I met ex-cons, meth cooks, Vietnam vets, gang members, drug addicts, survivors of sexual abuse in multiple churches, hard-right anti-government sovereign citizen types who showed me their huge collections of guns, all kinds of people.

I met a man who survived the Rwandan genocide, who

cried his eyes out, telling me about how his whole family was killed. I was 20 years old, at the beginning of my mission, and I was sitting there in his living room knowing there was nothing I could say to him. But this guy knew we were just a couple of kids, and he didn't expect us to be able to relate or to have anything useful to say. He just wanted someone to witness his pain. That was another thing I learned on my mission, how to just be there for people, knowing I can't solve their problems but I can listen. There's no point in looking at what someone else is going through and thinking, "that's too heavy, I can't deal with it," when they have no choice but to deal with it.

A sense of humour, some slight self-deprecation, and a sense of reality will go a long way to earning the trust of people who spend their lives trusting no one. People have told me those are some of my best qualities, and they came from the worst two years of my life.

growing up

I was born and raised in the Mormon church. My dad converted in his twenties, and my mother was born into it: her mother was a convert. I was indoctrinated from day one that I would be a missionary someday. When I look back, I can see that growing up in the church has caused me a lot of mental scarring. But when you're in it, you're just in it, and you don't know any different.

We moved around a lot, from Southern Ontario to Northern Ontario, and back. My dad's dad was in the Air Force, and my dad was an army brat who grew up everywhere. Because of that, he had itchy feet and wanted to move all the time. My dad liked the South, and my mom was from Sault Sainte Marie, and she liked living in the North.

I spent some of my formative years in a town in Northern Ontario called Balmertown, five hours west of Thunder Bay, literally at the end of the road. It's a rough, violent, racist place. I had tried following the rules and it didn't get me anywhere, so I started drinking to black out. I'd hitchhike home, not remembering how I got there.

A lot of the places we lived, we were the only Mormon family, so we'd hold church in our living room, just us. I was never a very good Mormon, though. One time the cops showed up in the middle of our living room church service because I'd been out drunk the other night and a friend ratted me out. The other guys I got drunk with all got charged with underage drinking, 'cause they admitted it, but I already knew to lie.

I doubt many a good Mormon kid can say they almost burned to death in an abandoned trailer park, while blackout drunk on whisky and stolen beer that tasted like a fish cooler, boom box blasting Korn's debut album. I heard the panic, saw the flames and rolled over and went back to sleep like it was just another Tuesday in the North. Norman Rockwell never painted that shit.

When I was growing up, my family moved, on average, every 18 months. And they didn't give a fuck about school schedules, so one time I started a new school two weeks before summer vacation.

When we lived places where there were other Mormons, church life was all-consuming. You could easily spend the whole weekend at church, with Young Men's or Young Women's activities on Wednesday nights, and early morning seminary at 6am before high school. It keeps you very busy. The church has a very us-versus-them mentality: you can't trust anyone who isn't in the church, you can't date anyone who isn't in the church, and you're always supposed to be trying to convert people who aren't members of the church, even when you're a kid. I never did that though: maybe I didn't love Jesus enough, but I was getting bullied all the time anyways. There you have it, Jesus cursed me 'cause I didn't suck his dick enough. Goddamn, what a cool guy I grew up worshiping, a real class act. Oh, and a bishop once told my dad I was destined for hell. That bishop raped one of my friends soooo… yeah. Cults are a fuckin' trip.

In two of the places we lived, Kitchener and Niagara Falls, my parents converted the attic of our house into an apartment to rent out to missionaries. Missionaries make perfect tenants, because the church pays their rent, and they have to be home by 9pm and in bed by 10. None of the missionaries ever stayed with us more than a few months, and mostly they were pretty boring, except that two of them got caught doing drugs, and one had a heating blanket that caught on fire in the night and burned holes through the bed.

So I grew up with missionaries around, and with the knowledge that this was what I would be doing later, and that I had no choice in that. It didn't even occur to me that it might be something I didn't want to do, until I was a year into my own mission.

cult

Mormonism is a cult. I mean, it's not a death cult, and it's a cult that's found a way to be very successful (200 billion dollars stashed away like it was couch change, total control of a U.S state, 15 million members, that kind of successful: Jim Jones cried himself to sleep wishing he had that kind of power). And like any cult, it has levels.

When you're eight years old, you get baptized. At 12, you go into the Young Men's or Young Women's program, and boys get the Aaronic priesthood. Then you can go do baptisms for the dead. At 18, boys get the Melchizedek priesthood, and women… well, women get married.

When you're 19, you get to do the rest of the secret ceremonies in the temple, which are, unfortunately, really fucking boring. But, you do get to learn the secret handshakes that will get you into heaven, so that's cool. That's also the point when you get the Magic Underwear. Which I was kind of excited about, because of course I was curious.

> **magic underwear**
>
> "A temple garment, also referred to as garments, the garment of the holy priesthood, or Mormon underwear, is a type of underwear worn by adherents of the Latter Day Saint movement after they have taken part in the endowment ceremony. Garments are required for any individual who previously participated in the endowment ceremony to enter a temple. The undergarments are viewed as a symbolic reminder of the covenants made in temple ceremonies and are seen as a symbolic and/or literal source of protection from the evils of the world."
>
> *"Temple garment," Wikipedia*

(It turns out the magic underwear is just hot, itchy, uncomfortable, and all-around a pain in the ass. And unless you have some kind of fetish for Mormonism, the garments are plain goddamn unsexy in every way.)

It's all set up to lead you along this path, with the ultimate goal of getting married in the temple after you do your mission. I'm married to my first wife in the temple, which isn't great, because if you get married in the temple, it's for eternity, so she and I, after we die, we're stuck together forever.

What it felt like to me, following these steps, was being in a river, and just being pushed along by the current. I felt like

I was doing good, doing all the right things, maybe even making my parents proud. It keeps your life very goal-oriented.

From age 12 on, every year, or whenever you want to do anything like go on a youth trip, you have to do worthiness interviews. You can't go to the temple without a recommend, which is like a card you carry to show you've been through this process. The worthiness interview is a one-on-one meeting with the bishop, where he asks you a bunch of personal questions: Do you masturbate? Do you look at pornography? Have you broken the word of wisdom? Are you honest to your fellow men? Do you tithe?

And of course, you're gonna lie to the dude. I hate to admit this, but the church taught me how to lie. If you go into a room with a bishop, you're gonna fucking learn how to lie really fast.

The Mormon church functions on shame: You grow up in a structure with strict rules that are almost impossible to follow-- no drinking, no smoking, no coffee, no tea, no sex outside of marriage, no masturbation. Since you can never follow all the rules, you grow up striving to be a worthy member of the church, but always falling short, and feeling constant shame.

missionary training center

Men are eligible to go on their mission once they are 19 and finished school. It's 21 for women, since they want to give them extra time to possibly get married. Then you start the application process.

After my mom died, my dad had just checked out. My older sister and I had to raise five kids, plus whoever else was hanging out at our place at the time. Have you ever met a sixteen year old who was just completely burnt out on life? That was me. I was shoplifting at 15 to be able to eat. I had to grow up really fast, but I also never really got to grow up.

By the time I was 17, I'd helped raised my family, I'd been through a lot. My aunt and uncle in Ottawa asked if I wanted to come live with them. My dad couldn't take care of me, and I knew there was no future for me in Northern Ontario, so I said yes. And it was from there that I left to go on my mission.

You apply to your bishop, and he and the guy above him have to sign off on it, and then your application goes to Salt Lake City. You have to go through a whole process of medical and dental checkups, because there's no health insurance on a mission. So I had to get all my wisdom teeth pulled first. Some drone looks at your application and assigns you to a location, which could be anywhere in the world. You get a letter in the mail that tells you where you're going, and when you have to report to the missionary training center, the MTC. I had friends go to Haiti, the Philippines, Madagascar, South Africa, England, all over the place.

That's how it usually works, anyways.

For me, I had a diagnosis of depression on my medical record, and this was a time when the church had just realized that mental illness is a thing. Right before I sent my application in, there had been a depressed missionary at the MTC who ran away in the middle of the night, and got hit and killed by a car. That made the church realize they should take mental health a bit more seriously, and I think nowadays if you have any mental health issues, they won't send you on a mission.

But back then, they didn't really know what to do, so they sent me to Montreal for a four-month probation period. My aunt and uncle drove me to Montreal, and I spent four months there before I got my official call. They figured they'd have me serve for a while close to home to see if I could hack it, then they gave me my real call, letting me know I'd be doing my mission in Tacoma, WA, and sent me off to the MTC.

As soon as I got to Salt Lake City I got VIOLENTLY ILL*, which was awkward as fuck, because I was staying at a family friend's place for a few days until I had to report to the MTC. Other people my age were traveling, going to parties, getting laid, having fun: meanwhile, I'm murdering the bathroom of some kind Mormons I'd never met before in Provo, Utah. At no point did I stop and think, "This isn't normal." Just another Monday working down at the cult mine.

It's amazing what people go through on their missions, and talk about it like it's normal. One of my friends got a foreskin infection while doing his mission in the Philippines. He had to get circumcised, and the doctor slit his foreskin lengthwise, pulled it down, and sewed it to the shaft like a banana. He told us this like any other missionary tells their war stories, as though it was on the same level as me getting terrible athlete's foot and pissing on my feet every morning to cure it. (It works, trust me!)

The MTC is a campus next to Brigham Young University (BYU). It's an extremely weird environment.

If you're doing an English-speaking mission like I was, you're there for three weeks. If you're doing your mission in a non-English-speaking area, you're there for about six weeks, doing language training. That's really not a long time to learn a new language, but if that's your situation, then you're not allowed to speak your first language. Even if you only know one word in the language you're learning,

*This reminds me: They will probably deny it if you ask, but trust me: almost every former missionary has at least one story of shitting their pants while serving the church. Honestly, I wish that was the zine I was writing for you, just a compilation of Mormon missionaries shitting themselves.

that's the word you're going to use. Apparently they use the military's language-training program. For Finnish, which is an incredibly hard language to learn, I've heard people say that the only people who can learn it that fast are either Finnish or Mormon.

> "The ties between the U.S. military and the MTC run pretty deep. The Army's Intelligence Brigade, made up of linguists, is based in Utah and draws on former missionaries to fill its ranks."
>
> *"Lessons From The Language Boot Camp For Mormon Missionaries", npr.org*

In the MTC, you're in a room with bunk beds. There's six of you living in this tiny room together, and you pray a lot. This was during the time when people were campaigning to take the Confederate flag off of state capitol buildings, and one time I heard this guy from Mississippi, a good ol' boy from the South, in the middle of his prayer, add in, "Dear God, don't let them take the flag off of the capitol building." George Bush also got elected while I was in the MTC, and everyone was cheering. Provo is really, really Republican.

It's really gender-segregated, and in the men's side, everyone showers in one big room full of poles with four shower heads coming out of them, that we called the Tree of Life. My friend told me that he had this one kid in his group who, every time they were all showering together, would soap up his butt and just spin around on the floor. I think the women's side had shower stalls, but the dudes didn't deserve any dignity, I guess.

You eat a lot of cheap, low-grade sugary food, like all-you-can-drink orange juice, then sit around all day, so everyone there gets horrible gas and farts constantly. The theory amongst missionaries was that the church put a drug in the food that took away your libido to prevent missionaries from fucking.

They did have a really good selection of cereal in the cafeteria, though. And ice cream sandwiches. So it wasn't all bad.

companions

Throughout your whole mission, you have a companion, and you have to stay within sight of your companion at all times. Even in the supermarket buying groceries. But they rotate your companion every couple of months, because they don't want people to get too close.

I think I had around 13 companions over my two-year mission: some I tolerated, some I loved, and some I despised. I had companions who'd rat me out if I like, took an extra hour at lunch to have a nap. Like, fuck you, dude. The guys I despised, I secretly read their journals to see if they were shit-talking me, and some were. People think punks are full of drama, but they've got nothing on missionaries.

Some of my companions were just so goddamned sheltered. Some of them had been homeschooled. And one time we were in a house and the guy had like a pound of weed on the coffee table, and my companion had no idea what it was. But I'd grown up in Northern Ontario, where drinking is the national pastime. When Facebook first started, I was part of a Facebook group called "I can't remember my weekends cause I grew up in Northern Ontario."

The worst was my first companion in Tacoma. He wasn't even an asshole, which at least would have been interesting. This guy was just so eager and all about the rules.

I couldn't deal with people who on my mission who were obsessed with rules, took themselves too seriously, and didn't have a sense of humor. 'Cause like, we're all miserable, we're all stuck doing this thing we don't want to do. Don't pretend you enjoy it.

Most of the people who were like that were from small-town Utah, though. The thing is, in the church, being a missionary is seen as special. And it's the first time in their lives a lot of these kids have ever been seen as anything special.

The missionaries I really hated were ones that were obsessed with numbers. And obsessed with the game. There's a few positions in the mission where a missionary can have power over other missionaries, and there's this weird jockeying for those few positions of power. If you're, like, the assistant to the president of the mission, you get to go wherever you want within the mission. I hated that shit though. I never wanted any responsibilities whatsoever.

Some people were great, though. In Montreal, I served with a guy named Elder Nate Nielsen, who was an active member of the US Marine Corps who was given leave to serve his mission. He was tough but also a ton of fun, and we got along great.

A year later, I was in Kent, WA, a town between Tacoma and Seattle. I got a new companion who looked awfully familiar, and an hour later I realized he looked just like Elder Nielsen and came from the same part of Utah. He turned out to be Curtis Nielsen, Nate's younger brother. He was a nurse, super kind, funny like his brother, and we became fast pals. Their mother bought me a new pair of shoes when Curtis told her that mine were worn out and I couldn't afford new ones or ask my family for help.

I hope Nate and Curtis are doing good. I think sometimes about how Nate would have been the perfect age to end up in the War on Terror, and I hope he is OK. His family had been through enough, they didn't need the horrors of the past twenty years thrown in there.

I didn't keep in touch with any of my friends from my mission: to me, it was a lightning in a bottle. For the time we were together, I knew them and I loved them. But I never knew, or wanted to know how they would see me after my mission or who I am now. I'd rather not spoil the few good memories I had from that time.

the rules

When you're on your mission, you're basically cut off from the entire world. There's an insane amount of rules. You can't read anything except the scriptures and the missionary training manual. You can't watch TV. You can't listen to the radio. No chewing gum.

Every zone has a leader, and you give your numbers to your district leader. They call you to make sure you're home. So there's always somebody checking on where you are. They check your odometer on your car to make sure you're not taking trips.

You have to sleep in the same room as your companion, but you can't sleep in the same bed: that's in the rule book.

You wake up at six, and study for three hours. Fucking boring. I would always fall asleep when I was supposed to be doing Bible study. I could not stay awake. Then you have companionship study where you and your companion practice door approaches or shit like that.

First thing when you wake up, you pray. When you leave your house, you say a prayer. When you start your car, you say a prayer. Eat dinner, you pray. End of the day, you pray. You fucking pray so much. I hated it.

And then you go out and do tracking, which is knocking on doors. In the Seattle mission, we had to do it minimum five hours a day. It's brutal. I still hate the rain to this day, because I spent so much time walking in the rain in Seattle. As soon as I feel the drops hitting my back, I'm right back there.

And then you have to be back in your apartment by 9:30 and in bed by 10, six days a week.

Mondays are what we called PT days. You have from 6 am to 6:30 pm to do laundry, grocery shop, and it's the only day you're allowed to write letters. The other missionaries always wanted to get together on their PT days and play goddamn basketball, cause they're all Utah jocks. I hated it.

There's also a rule that when you're a missionary and someone gives you food, you have to eat all of it, so that you don't insult anyone. No matter how gross it is, you have to eat it. One time I was served something that I thought was creamed corn that turned out to just be extremely lumpy gravy, and I still ate all of it. And Jello! I don't know why, but Mormons fucking love Jello and I've eaten probably every configuration of Jello you could think of.

When I did my mission, in the early 2000s, you couldn't have a cell phone. You couldn't access computers. No emailing. Nowadays, missionaries actually have cell phones, and they're allowed to send emails home. But they still can't make phone calls. You get like an hour on Christmas and Mother's Day to call home, that's all. Two times each year, so four times total.

My brother served his mission at the same time as me, in the B.C., Canada, mission, and my cousin served in Long Beach, California. We didn't see each other for three years, but my brother and I actually did break the rules and call each other and leave prank messages on each other's voicemail.

You're also not allowed to swim on your mission. My brother had broken both his collarbones as a kid, and when he was on his mission he had to get special permission to be able to swim for physiotherapy, and his companion had to sit in the bleachers the whole time and watch him.

All my life, I'd always known missionaries couldn't swim. And I love swimming. I grew up in the North, swimming in lakes as a kid. I always thought it was so weird that there was this doctrine that missionaries can't swim. There's this idea floating around in the church that missionaries aren't allowed to swim because Satan has dominion over the water. It wasn't until my mission that I learned the real reason they can't swim is the church doesn't have insurance to cover it.

At the end of every week, you and your companion have a talk about the past week, go over your numbers, and then you are supposed to do "compliments and stompliments", and tell each other three things you like about them, and three things that irritate you or that you think they need to improve. It's extremely awkward and weird. Like, these were the people I was dealing with: I'm amazed I made it through the whole two years.

staying human

Mormonism tries really hard to erase your whole identity, especially while you are on mission. You lose your whole sense of self for two years and become a drone. All you're supposed to think about is church work, and even if you're in a big city, you're completely cut off from the rest of the world, your family and friends, and all of your personal interests.

You're supposed to just think about the people you meet as numbers. You keep track of how many doors you knock, how many seemed interested, how many invited you back, how many lessons you taught.

You wear a nametag with your last name, and "Elder" if you're a guy, "Sister" if you're a girl. People don't even know each other's first names. But the thing I find interesting about it is that it's impossible to take someone's identity away completely, they will always find ways to make it show. If you turn over a missionary's nametag and look at the back, everyone has stickers on theirs, as a little way of preserving their personality.

The best advice my mom ever gave me, is that if you don't get a sense of humour, the world will crush you. Humour and honesty are what got me through my mission, the ability to laugh at shit.

There's a perception in the church that missionaries are very dignified, and you're supposed to try to maintain that perception, but you're teenagers, about 19 to 22, and knocking on doors is really boring. So you make up games to try and make it fun, like how many times can you say "meow" while talking to someone at the door, or how many times can you insult them without them noticing.

In the time I was on my mission, all the other missionaries had borderline pathological obsessions with quoting The Simpsons, the Chris Farley movie *Tommy Boy* (and also his SNL character Matt Foley), and *The Princess Bride* (Mormons love that movie for whatever reason).

When you're knocking on doors, you usually alternate which of you does the talking. Sometimes the person who isn't talking will flick their companion in the balls immediately before the person opens their door, then they have to try and keep their composure while they do their speech.

There was a similar thing we'd do, if we were at a family's house praying with them, where your companion would put your hand on your knee while you were praying out loud, and then move their hand up and up your thigh to see if they could get you to panic and mess up the prayer.

Two other more human moments during my mission

where the Mormon script was interrupted were the day a magnitude 6.5 earthquake hit Seattle, and 9/11.

We were out knocking doors in the suburbs during the earthquake, and we didn't know what to do, so we just kept knocking on doors. The first person who answered basically said, "There was just an earthquake, what the fuck are you doing here?" and we were like, "Yeah, OK, fair."

One morning, the zone leader knocks on our door and said, "the World Trade Centre just exploded." I called my mission president, and he told me not to bother knocking on any doors that day, but to find a member I liked and go watch TV with them. 9/11 caused a lot of strange shifts: devout people becoming atheists, people I never thought would go to church that started going every Sunday.

I did get to meet and spend time with some families I really loved cause they reminded me of my family: kind of poor, loud, obnoxious, messy, families where the kids fought constantly, and the parents fought in front of us at the dinner table, and they had too many kids and not enough money, but they made do.

Those kinds of families reminded me of a home that I'd had that had disintegrated years before my mission, and I could never go back to. So I always gravitated to low-income, abrasive, working class, big, loud families, who never seemed to get along, but if you talked shit about any of them, the whole family would kick the shit out of you.

cognitive dissonance

When you knock on someone's door, you usually give a pre-planned lesson. When they answer the door, you say, "Hi, my name is Elder Reid, I'm from the Church of Jesus Christ of Latter Day Saints. Would you have a moment to hear a message about Jesus Christ and his plan for us on this earth and the restoration of his true religion on this earth?"

I remember the first time I said it, when I was in Montreal, and I had a clear and distinct thought run through my head that it was bullshit. But it wasn't a good time to be struggling with cognitive dissonance, so I didn't end up leaving the church until I was 28, after having a kid and getting divorced.

Missionaries have a whole program for converting people, and they even sometimes call it "the manipulation pattern". It's no wonder I felt so much cognitive dissonance.

And then there's being a trans woman who came out years later. When I look back on it, how do I reconcile who I was then with who I am now? I don't know how to think about the rule that you can't have any contact with anyone of the opposite sex. Because when I look back on it now, I was constantly around men, "the opposite sex." I was always jealous of the sister missionaries because I just wanted to hang out with them.

As a Mormon missionary, when you have someone who's interested in getting baptized, you have a little laminated card you take out, that has a series of questions you have to ask them. If they answer yes to any of them, and they don't have to tell you which one is a yes, then you have to send them to the highest authority in your ward. The two questions that always stuck out to me were, "Have you ever had a homosexual relationship?" and "Have you ever thought about getting elective transsexual surgery?" Try reading that out loud to people as a Mormon missionary and a closeted trans woman. Yeah, that's my life.

Mormons are all about personal responsibility, thinking of things in terms of systematic oppression is something they completely can't do. If I try to say anything to the Mormons in my life about fucked up homophobic and transphobic things that leaders have said, they just won't even be able to hear it.

When I mention to an active member, someone who still goes to church, that I still have trauma around growing up in a church that hates trans people, they always say that they don't remember anything. They don't remember church leaders ever saying anything about gay or trans people, whereas I saw every little thing.

I spent so much of my life pretending to be someone I wasn't. And now I struggle when I have to do that in any way.

When you leave a cult, you feel really gullible and stupid. And now, after that, it's hard for me to believe in anything, in any kind of spirituality. I don't judge people for believing, but I can't do it. But when you're in it, when you're a missionary, you don't think for yourself, you don't think about the bigger picture. You don't think about how fucked up it is. 'Cause you're doing God's work. And God doesn't make mistakes (except me).

class & money

I grew up with a strong awareness of class and poverty, from spending my formative years in small towns in Northern Ontario.

It's a place that's very working-class and very based around the union. In one town I lived in, the miners went on strike for four years. When I walked to school in the morning, I'd be walking past the front gates of this mine, with a bunch of miners standing around barrel fires, drinking bottles of whiskey, and yelling at scabs.

When you're a missionary, you pay $12,000 to the church before you leave, and the church puts that into a pot and gives it back to the missionaries over the course of the mission. In one of the areas I was living, my companion and I didn't get enough money to eat. We were lucky we happened to have a bread maker, because the last week of the month we were eating nothing but bread, or relying on people inviting us over for dinner.

Mormon missionaries usually spend a lot of time in poor areas. More people are interested there, because when you're in a desperate situation, you'll try anything. In rich areas, you won't get any numbers. But during my mission, a leader from Utah came and gave us a lecture, and told us to stop converting so many poor people, because it was a burden on the church. It really pissed me off, because money shouldn't have any meaning within a religion. If someone is struggling, you fucking help them out.

But the church just doesn't like poor people, and it's just getting worse and worse. More and more people are falling into the Prosperity Doctrine way of thinking, the idea that the more money you give to God, the more blessings you get. If you have money, it means you're a good person, and if you're poor, it's your fault.

Joseph Smith, who founded Mormonism, rose through the ranks of the Masons pretty fast, ditched them, then ripped off their rituals in the Mormons' temple ceremony. He was a con man. And the church is still conning.

The church took a billion dollars of tithe money from people in Canada, and gave it to BYU: money that was supposed to be used to help out poor and struggling people here.

The Mormon church is the largest land owner in Florida. They own a 300,000 acre cattle ranch. They own 2% of the land in the state, and they're the fifth-largest land owner in the United States. They have tons of other investments nobody knows about.

I was in a meeting one time with some ward leaders, talking about filling out a cheque. And I've always remembered how the the bishop said, "Don't worry, church checks never bounce."

"[In] the last 15 years, the LDS church in Canada has moved more than $1 billion across the border to Brigham Young universities in the U.S., an investigation by CBC's The Fifth Estate has found."

"The majority of that money came from tithing — or the 10 per cent of gross annual income some 200,000 Canadian Mormons… contribute to the church annually."

"Mormon Church in Canada moved $1B out of the country tax free — and it's legal," CBC.

• • •

"For more than half a century, the Mormon Church quietly built one of the world's largest investment funds. Almost no one outside the church knew about it."

"The Mormon Church Amassed $100 Billion. It Was the Best-Kept Secret in the Investment World," Wall Street Journal.

• • •

"The Church of Jesus Christ of Latter-day Saints and a nonprofit entity that it controlled have been fined $5 million by the Securities and Exchange Commission over accusations that the religious institution failed to properly disclose its investment holdings.

In an order released Tuesday, the SEC alleged that the church illicitly hid its investments and their management behind multiple shell companies from 1997 to 2019. In doing so, it failed to disclose the size of the church's equity portfolio to the SEC and the public."

"Feds fine Mormon church for illicitly hiding $32 billion investment fund behind shell companies," NBC News

hard right

The Mormon church has so many ties to the hard right. They didn't let Black people fully join the church til the '70s, and they still hate gay and trans people to this day.

> "From the mid-1800s to 1978, Mormonism's largest denomination, the Church of Jesus Christ of Latter-day Saints (LDS Church) barred Black women and men from participating in ordinances of its temples necessary for the highest level of salvation, prevented most men of Black African descent from being ordained to the church's lay, all-male priesthood, supported racial segregation in its communities and schools, taught that righteous Black people would be made White after death, and opposed interracial marriage. The temple and priesthood racial restrictions were lifted by top leaders in 1978. In 2013 the church disavowed its previous teachings on race for the first time."
>
> *"Black people and Mormonism," Wikipedia*

In the '80s, there was an anti-communist white power terrorist cell called the Silent Brotherhood in the Pacific Northwest that was started by a Mormon. They robbed banks and armored cars and assassinated a Jewish radio host. Eventually the FBI cornered the leader and burned him alive in his cabin.

The CIA and the FBI and the US military love Mormons[*]. When I was on my mission in the U.S. after the invasion of Afghanistan had started, Marines and soldiers would always come up and try and recruit us. The CIA and the FBI recruit tons of Mormons. Bruce Jessen, one of the CIA psychologists who created the "enhanced interrogation techniques" that were used to torture CIA detainees, is a Mormon. You will never see dick riding the way the Mormon Church rides America's dick.

Here's the thing: if you think that your religion is the one true religion, it gives you carte blanche to do anything, because, well, I've got God on my side. The church is full of fraud and abuse, including sexual abuse. When I look back on it, it seems so dark, but when I was in it, I thought it was just the way the world worked.

---

[*] *"Why Mormons Make Great FBI Recruits", Atlas Obscura*

punk

Growing up in Northern Ontario taught me to distrust authority from day one: don't listen to the boss, don't talk to cops.

And growing up Mormon just drove that point home. From the age of 10, every year I had to go in front of the bishop for a worthiness interview. So I was still a kid when I learned how to lie to authority, because there's no way I'm gonna tell some 40 year old that I jerk off. Mormon scriptures say that all liars get sent straight to hell, but everyone in the church lies: they want you to lie.

So growing up hating authority primed me to get into punk. I got into metal through my sister, and then into Nirvana, and then into punk from there. It spoke to me because it was music for young, angry, poor people, and I was a young, angry, poor person.

Growing up Mormon also really prepared me to be in punk and queer scenes, because it's a small community with SO MUCH GOSSIP. I've had punk friends say, "I can't stand all the gossip, how do you deal with it?" And I tell them, I grew up in the gossip.

Even though punk is morally and ehtically the opposite of Mormonism, they have a lot in common. Small, insular communities full of radicals and moderates, an us-vs.-them mentality, esoteric information and language, lots of infighting, cliques, bitching, shit-talking, backstabbing, and gossip. Punks are mostly on the right side of history, and are way more open about how fucked-up and traumatized we are, so they aren't one and the same, but it makes sense that I'd so easily fall from one and slip into the other.

Not long after I left the church, the maintenance guy at my work saw me wearing a Dead Kennedys shirt. I was a poser who didn't even listen to the Dead Kennedys, but he saw the shirt, asked me if I was a punk, and invited me to a show.

I'd been into punk since I was a teenager, but it was my first basement show, and the first time I'd actually been plugged into the community instead of just listening to the music (although I never did get into the Dead Kennedys, I think they're annoying).

When I started going to house shows, people would come up and talk to me, and I realized they didn't have to. They weren't going to gain anything by talking to me, and they weren't trying to convert me.

I lost one social circle but fell right into another. And I know now how lucky I am in that. A lot of people, when they leave the church, are just alone and abandoned. I know a lot of people make fun of the saying "punk rock saved my life", but it literally saved my life.

post-mormon life

I got married not long after my mission, when I was 25. Because that's what you do when you come home from a mission: you get married. People thought I'd be a bachelor for life, and they were praying for me to get married. I never thought I'd get married either. Then I met my first wife, we fell in love, and got married six months later.

We were married for three years, and I was in way over my head. The first time I held our kid, all I could think was that I had no fucking clue what I was doing.

She came home one day and told me that she didn't love me anymore and kicked me out. I ended up homeless, it was rough. For a long time, we never talked without fighting. But recently she sent me a picture of our kid. He's 17 now, and he's beautiful, and he's doing good.

If I saw a picture like that even a couple of years ago, I would have become incredibly depressed or angry, or felt guilty about all the time I missed, but now I'm able to be glad that he's doing good, and grateful to his mom for holding it down, and just hope that someday he and I can have a relationship.

•••

The reason I stayed faithful to the church for so long is because there's a doctrine that if you're righteous, you can be with your family forever. And my mom died when I was 15. We put her in the ground, and then the next day we were back in school and nobody ever talked about it.

I tried to do everything a Mormon was supposed to do: I tried to be a good husband, a good man. I was full of doubts that I did my best to ignore. But when you repress things, they don't stay down. You gotta keep pushing them, and it takes so much fucking energy to do that. It's sad, and it's exhausting.

The doubts just kept coming, because nothing in my life went the way it was supposed to. The promise is, if you're a good Mormon, you'll be rewarded. You'll be blessed. And I saw it happening for other people. All my Mormon friends who are even close to my age, they all have houses, partners, great careers. I am so far behind them, and it really gets me down sometimes. But then I also realize that I know stuff about the world that they don't, and when the world turns upside down, they're gonna need someone who can navigate that: that'll be me.

The moments that lead to me leaving the church were small and anticlimactic. The first was just a time that I was in a sacrament meeting at church. I looked around, and I thought:

1. All these people think they're going to heaven.
2. I can't stand 90% of these people, they're all assholes.
3. I don't want to be with these people for eternity.

I was with my second wife at the time, but I didn't talk to her about it because if your partner is active in the church, and you leave the church, they will leave you.

There's a subreddit called r/ExMormon, where people who have left the church talk about their experiences. It's often sad, and it's often funny, too. There are a lot of full-blown adults who have never drunk alcohol and want advice on how to try drinking for the first time, or who get drunk for the first time as adults and have a really messy time.

The second moment that lead to me leaving the church was when I just left a tab open one day with the r/ExMormon subreddit open, and my wife saw it, and said, "You read it too?" and I told her I did, and she said, "The people there are right." I asked her, "Are we going to church this week?" and she said, "Nope." And we just stopped.

"Two-hundred and seventy-eight participants were recruited primarily through LDS-affiliated LGBTQQA support and discussion groups on Facebook... A majority of participants (89.2%) likely met criteria for PTSD diagnosis related to their religious experiences."

"Unlike other trauma that occurs in relationship to distinct events or incidents, spiritual trauma often involves long-term exposure – sometimes from birth – to messages and beliefs that can impair mental health...Individuals who are born into a religious environment might find those teachings and beliefs become influential as they develop views of themselves and the world. Additionally, unlike otherforms of trauma where the individual may have the ability to potentially escape or defend themselves from the abuser, spiritual trauma includes concepts of God, "who has all knowledge, all power, and is present everywhere," thus the spiritually abused may feel they have no escape."

Coming Out Mormon: An Examination Of Religious Orientation, Spiritual Trauma, And PTSD Among Mormon And Ex-Mormon LGBTQQA Adults, Brian William Simmons

accept yourself or die

When I came out to my family as trans, they talked about it like, "you were one person, and now you're another person."

And even to me, in some ways it felt like it came out of nowhere. I had buried it so deep I'd forgotten it was even there. I learned so long ago, probably before I could even talk, that there were parts of me I could never express. When I was a little kid, I loved *Anne of Green Gables*, I loved *Little Women*… but when I was in grade 9, I also watched a bunch of kids my age beat a homeless guy nearly to death. What do you think they would have done to me if I said, "Hey, by the way, I'm a girl?"

My ex studied linguistics, and she taught me the idea that the language you use shapes your reality. I never knew the word "trans" growing up, or had any trans heroes to look up to.

The first time I ever remember seeing anyone queer in my life was in Red Lake, Ontario, when I was in grade 9. I was in an empty hallway and two older girls walked by holding hands. One of them turned around, and said to me, in an extremely Northern Ontario way, "What the fuck are you looking at? You never seen a couple of dykes before?" I still think of those two girls to this day, but suffice to say I didn't have a lot of chances to see queer and trans people while I was growing up.

When I left the church, all the gender stuff started coming to the surface. My wife and I were the supers of a huge apartment building, and there were lots of empty apartments. So I'd just borrow some of my wife's clothes, find an empty apartment, and live out my trans girl fantasies for hours.

And then we had our kid, who I stayed home with, and it was the best year of my life. But at the same time, I was going back and forth, constantly. I went through the same thing most trans people go through, beating ourselves up, wondering "Am I really trans? Am I trans enough?" If you're asking, you most likely are. I went through the whole thing, "Am I trans? No, I'm just a crossdresser. OK, maybe I'm trans, but I'll never be accepted as a woman, because I'm not feminine enough."

It got to a point eventually, where I realized I had to just accept it or die. My wife and our kid went away for the weekend, and I had a really terrible weekend, and I finally realized: I want to see my kid grow up. I grew up without a mother, and it sucks. It's better to survive.

So I made up my mind to tell my wife, but I waited too long, and she found out by checking my Reddit history (yes, the second big change in my life that happened via me leaving Reddit open), and she just asked me, "Are you a girl?"

It was a massive relief to finally be out, but I also had no road map. I'd repressed it for so long, and the gates were finally open.

My wife and I separated right away. Sexuality is a spectrum for some people, but she, bless her heart, is straight straight straight. Not a hater, just 100% straight.

I came out to people over Messenger, mostly. I read that there has been research that people with borderline personality disorder, like me, can actually recognize negative emotions on people's faces faster than people without BPD. It's a horrible skill. They call it the Empathy Paradox, because people with BPD have so much empathy, but we often use it looking for signs of rejection or any other kind of negative emotion. And even if someone was ultimately supportive, I didn't want to see their first reaction when I told them.

I don't really engage a lot publicly as a trans person. I don't go to the trans march or things like that. But word got around that there was an older trans woman in the punk scene, and suddenly all these younger trans people were looking to me for help and advice. I try to help them. I've answered a lot of messages in the middle of the night from people in crisis.

I respect all the many types of struggles people have in their life, but I have a special place in my heart for trans women. Anyone who comes out as a trans women is hard as fuck. The world makes you pay a huge price for being who you are. I'm poor, I'm mentally ill, I've lost so much, and sometimes I wonder if it was worth it.

But at the same time, I get to be me. There's a lot of people in the world who never get that privilege. So many people are pretending to be someone they aren't. I've learned so much. I have friendships I never thought I'd have.

It's been a weird fucking journey. I'm three years older now that my mom was when she died, and I realized that she had no fucking clue what she was doing. She was as scared as I am, and there's something comforting in that: just realizing that none of us know what we're doing.

about the author

Imogen Reid is a photographer and artist in Ottawa, ON.

You can find her on Instagram at @dykeposerbitch.

about sheer spite press

Sheer Spite Press was founded in 2024 by Lee Pepper to publish and distribute useful, generous, personal, political, funny, heart-filled works. This is the very first book published by Sheer Spite, and I'm very proud of it!

The press shares work in three ways:

- Publishing work under the Sheer Spite Press name (like this book!)
- Print zine and book distribution
- Digital zine and book distribution

Get in touch if you'd like to collaborate!

www.sheerspite.ca
Instagam: @sheerspite
Email: lee@sheerspite.ca

Flip over for another book!

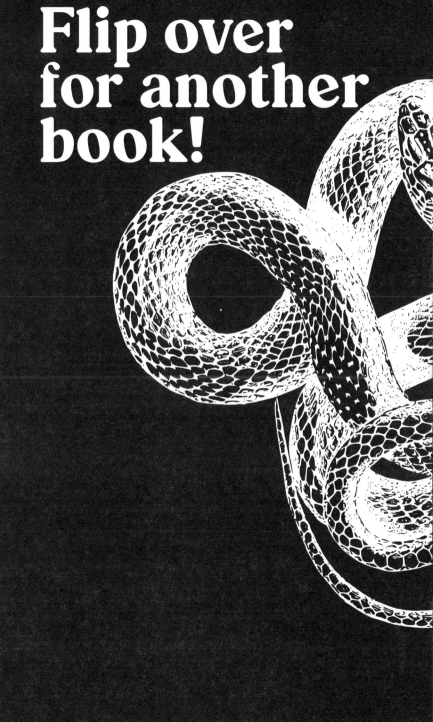

about the author

Kat Rogue is a writer and artist in Ottawa.

She chooses to be kind as often as possible despite carrying a deep well of fury in her chest.

You can find her fiction on Gumroad and AO3.

It would've been near impossible to create this zine without the amazing help from Lee Pepper, who did the art, layout, and inspired me to write. Thanks also to my writing pal Alanna Why, Renée Yoxon for helping get me into journaling in the first place, and to Alison for helping keep me alive.

This zine was inspired by a tweet I saw that basically said "all crossdressers are men," which hurt my feelings.

Envelope reads: For Myself, When I Need It

Dear future you,

I do not envy myself the journey I am about to undertake. There are perilous emotional and monetary costs. As of now I do not know where the journey ends, only that I know with precision that it must be initiated. There is at my front a ragged precipice. Every foothold and hand placement leads to the risk of falling to a bitter end, or cracked bones back at the start. Scrapes heal and each drop of blood is a false truth unlearned.

People come and go at the pace people come and go at. My cliff reads a different calendar; human relationships are a sneeze. There are boundless victories and unlimited setbacks. Last minute solutions lead to dead ends where climbing down would seem like failure to casual onlookers. The wall pays no mind. The further the stone roughens my grip, the less I care. Some go further and throw rocks. Razor sharp as they are, I am sharper still. I learn to love the climb.

Nearing the edge, you may be reminded why this all started. Or you won't. Try to remember, it's vital lest we reach the wrong peak. I have only the vaguest of sensations what it might look like, but I have goals on the feeling. A lightness not felt even by the still air. Planes have never flown so high. Clouds will envy you.

It is an ascension built just for you because only you can climb it. That's what makes it so difficult, but that is also why it is so attainable.

If you ever need help, I'll always be there. Just look in the mirror, love.

only become more complicated as time goes on. Don't let the fallacy of progress trick you. It can all be taken away.

Now, I'd like to end by transcribing a letter I hand-wrote for myself on September 12th, 2015. I was on the hormones waitlist for a month by that point and thought I'd be on estrogen before Halloween. No one told me I'd be waiting another 50 weeks. I gushed out my anger and resolve for the times to come when I knew I'd be too fucking down to know how to continue. I was bitter as hell about some things that I don't necessarily feel so strongly about anymore, but I won't edit those parts out. Thanks for reading.

The Future is Now. Shit!

Things are great now, aren't they? The internet is a veritable utopia of access to information for people all over the world. Transphobia is over!

Or, that's what I thought was supposed to happen. We have more tools than ever to teach the world about our oppression, but transphobes have the same ability to undermine that work. And they're good at it. Some of our progress feels more like sidegrades than upgrades. The more I listen to elders, the more it feels like we've traded our public spaces for legislative rights. Those things are great, of course! But, we need to be careful how quickly our IRL spaces can be taken from us if we don't physically show up for them.

Netflix and video games are niiiceee thooooo and going outside suuuuccckks and street harassment makes me wanna dieeeee. Hey, I played the WoW beta and used to run a Minecraft channel on YouTube. I get it! Bedroom computer time is important. But in a zine that praises the internet, I would be remiss not to mention the fact that it is being weaponized against us and that relationship will not just call it that? Don't you think trans women are women? Do you think crossdressing men should be able to access LGBT spaces and march in Pride? It sounds like you're saying autogynephelia is real?!?"

My answer to that would be that those questions are not being made in good faith so shut the hell up about it.

that people of all genders can take part it in in the ways that work best for them, to pick up and put back down again as they please. Less, "I am crossdressing" and more, "I am taking part in the act of crossdressing as it pertains to the freeing of my mind, body, and soul." The terms and definitions have transitioned ;) to encompass something greater.

Are my crossdressing days over? Welllllll, sort of. My trans girl aesthetics and my crossdressing aesthetics are totally dif and come out in different scenarios. Last month I just got this urge to pull off some CD action, so I put on my wig and lots of makeup and short dress and pump heels and stuffed my bra and it feels completely different from my everyday shit, even my slutty trans shit. If I went out in public dressed like that, I'd face harassment in ways I don't experience in everyday girl mode, in part because my girl mode takes passing and safety into consideration in ways my CD aesthetic does not. That's why I feel so warmly towards CDing. It's a more honest expression of my desires that puts the considerations of others and taboos completely aside. Like, for sure, for all intents and purposes, me being on estrogen and my legal name being Katalina is definitely breaking a taboo, but that taboo is being more and more accepted in a way dressing like a slutty crossdresser is not.

"But, Kat!", you may be asking, "If a cis woman wore articles of clothing in the style of crossdressing aesthetic as you've laid out, would she be crossdressing? What you're describing just sounds more like sexy boudoir stuff, why with customers and my coworkers still misgender me once a week. Legal name change and being allowed access to hormones took over a year of active waiting. I'm fretting over the myriad of trans surgeries I might have access to and get really sad when I realize how much money it all costs. Is that crossdressing and forced femme stories? Nah. That's boring, everyday girl stuff. Crossdressing is a fantastical mindset. You're sexy! gorgeous! naughty! desirable! It's fun and nasty and wrong and right and exhilarating. Crossdressing is the high fantasy version of my gender where I experience the best parts in shimmering technicolour on the adrenaline of fear and glory.

Closeted trans women who crossdress to stave off existential dread are different from crossdressing men. Trans women and cis men are so often lumped together because our bodies are born with some similar characteristics and then misidentified via lazy fucking medicine. Crossdressing is its own thing. It started as a verb to describe the act of wearing clothes and acting outside one's (euro-colonial) prescribed binary gender norms. When queer theory starts to break down those norms, or idealize breaking those norms, it can feel reductive or even dangerous to keep around a term like crossdressing because it continues to imply the presence of male-assigned bodies in clothes that weren't made for them, that clothing can even be gendered, and what we're trying to do is liberate trans women here, aren't we?! Break the binary?! I think it's better to frame crossdressing not as a verb, but as an activity and culture of its very own making note of fashion trends you see in public, paying attention to friends as they apply their own makeup.

Crossdressing is also a thing I couldn't do forever. The secrecy damaged my brain. The dissonance of over the top happiness to extreme dumpy sadness. The pretending. Despite it all, I learned what gender euphoria looked like. It taught me what working towards a goal looked like. How to work hard. It taught me patience. It taught me what passion meant. As a kid and young adult, people kept asking me "what do you wanna do with your life?" and "what are you passionate about?" I'd look at people around who knew they wanted to be doctors or athletes, and the only thing I knew for certain was "I'm a crossdresser."

I've seen cis people talk about gender euphoria through life milestones like getting married or buying a house. This isn't even a dig at cis people! It's just a thing I've noticed. Sometimes it's goofy things like Nail Clippers But For Men, other times it's sweet like, "I never felt more like a man than the first time I held my baby". That's really beautiful! Just, for me, I never felt more like a woman until I found myself on my knees in front of a mirror, legs splayed, staring at the shape of myself with lipstick stained teeth, zoned out and breathing heavy, cum dripping onto the torn pantyhose I stole from Walmart as the walls of dark shame slowly overcome my field of vision. To each their own, I fucking guess.

When I go to work or do groceries and my name is Kat and my pronouns are she and her and I generally pass people get to experience themselves. In general, I blame TERFS, gatekeepers, and violent transphobia for the ways we're unable to experience the human experience of gender. Those people have issues.

I went through different phases of 1) how I wanted to identify and 2) whether the ways I'd previous identified myself both outwardly and privately had any bearing on my legitimacy on how I did want to identify. And that's a big part of gatekeeping. It teaches us how to gatekeep ourselves so medical and governmental institutions don't have to. Like how in an abusive relationship you end up pre-gaslighting yourself to avoid worse, external abuse. Brains love survival techniques. By orienting myself as "just a crossdresser", or worse, "a disgusting crossdresser", I was able to sidestep the real issue of this girl is repressed as hell.

Knowing this and accepting it has also been helpful when it comes to understanding that crossdressing aesthetic is FUN AND COOL AS HELL and something to be admired and something to strive for. Crossdressing is the act of understanding the consequences of what you like and fucking doing it because god damn it feels so good and nobody's gettin' hurt. Wigs are fun. Putting on lots of makeup is fun. Dressing up all glamorous in your own damn house is fun, even for an audience of one. Seeing yourself in the mirror and just vibrating from head to toe in adrenaline and knowing that all your hard work has paid off just for this moment. Hard work like procuring your items, sneakily looking at makeup books in Chapters,

Crossdressing Is A Worthy Goal

There were some bad resources online in the 2000's as well. I don't want to give that shit any space here, but it had a lot to do with centering of cis women's feelings about their partners crossdressing or wanting to be women being bad and embarrassing and laughable. All this information befuddled my young mind. So, if some crossdressers are men, and others are closeted trans women, does that make them trans women used-to-be-male-crossdressers, or just young women expressing themselves as themselves in the only ways they could??

And my answer to that is: I don't care.

I really don't care if some trans women identify their past as "when I was a man" or "when I was a crossdresser" or "I was born a trans girl". They're all correct, because I'm not the fucking gender police. We can tend to want the exact same experience across the board instead of just standing in solidarity with each other's multitudes. Phrasing something as "all crossdressers are men" invalidates the complexities inherent in gender. It does a disservice to gender as a concept and the full breadth of how trans dispensing advice (I never posted tho, something I regret!). I was also aware of trans subreddits, but stayed away. So when my favourite posters left r/crossdressing one at a time to transition and that you could find them "on r/transgender", I followed. I began searching out other trans subreddits like r/transpassing, r/asktransgender, and most importantly, r/transtimelines. That last one is a subreddit where trans folks post before and after photos, usually with regards to hormone timelines. This is when I start learning about hormones in more detail. I currently follow a few trans women on other social media who posted to r/crossdressing wayyy back. Keeping ties with my roots.

r/crossdressing is really where it all came together for me because I saw people who were like me take that plunge forward. I wanted to plunge forward, too, I always wanted more, but I didn't have the resources or support to do that. I had so few examples of people who went from crossdressing into "I'm a girl actually" territory, but those numbers were growing. Thank you for everything, r/crossdressing.

anything: how to pass, crossdressing websites and stores, the few online resources we had, talking to partners, etc. The juxtaposition of sad posts where someone's partner disapproves of their dressing to others whose partners are supportive. There were also rare posts titled something like "first time crossdresser" and even where someone said they were looking for advice on how to "get into crossdressing". I read that and was like, what? "get into"? Like a hobby? I couldn't conceive of it being anything other than an utter and total compulsion one enacted from childhood.

Reddit is also where I first found Jessica Who HD. She made YouTube videos about the foibles of crossdressing, like managing multiple wigs and covering beard shadow. Before her I didn't know you could dress like that and also be so silly and fun. She has since deleted her account and I really miss knowing how she's doing. It would be cool to find out someday, but if I don't that is ok too! #privacy

Early crossdressing videos on YouTube were a lot of "shopping at the store" or "taking a drive in the country" and someone all dressed up walks into frame and poses next to her car as the wind crackles the audio. Some of these are still around and it's so nice. These expressions and public explorations of self are some of the most tender things I devoured growing up in the early YouTube era.

Every once in awhile there'd be the "it's more than dressing" post. These ones caught my eye and were eventually what helped me break. I had gotten to know these people, I went from lurker to full on commenter practicing scales before a piano lesson. The cold, dark evenings of an Ottawa autumn were the perfect setting for my bolder outings, especially around Halloween, which gave me the confidence of being potentially "caught". Head to toe transformations that took the entire evening to prep: the wig, the makeup, the stockings, the heels. Strolling around Centretown shivering with fear and adrenaline, really practicing my strut and devouring the click-clack of pumps on the pavement, pumps that fit. I suddenly started to care about selfies.

We're no longer partners, but continued to live as roommates for the first years of my transition and I consider her my chosen family. This took an immense amount of work on both of our parts.

Eventually, Aubrey's Place wasn't enough. I needed more. At 19 I did my first and only purge, throwing out a wig and a skirt I'd bought. I read about "purging" (throwing out all your girl stuff in an act of "I will never do this again!" hint: it never works) on the subreddit, r/crossdressing. It got to the point where I looked at every single post in the subreddit's history, feverishly refreshing the front page everyday for more. I memorized the usernames of those I had crushes on. A lot of those early photos were on low res cameras. A few didn't include the person's face. A common crossdressing photo is the waist down shot with stockings and heels chilling out on a couch, or simple bathroom mirror selfies. But in so many you can see the happiness bursting through, the smiles, the exhilaration of reading and liking posts from first timers. Threads were open to myself up for weeks to visit Walmart to buy or steal basic makeup. Foundation helped obscure the parts of my face I hated the most. I would apply my makeup in heels while the apartment was all mine. This was also the first time I could stomp around in heels outside of a bathroom without fear of being discovered. I had my own laptop and would search for trans porn and look at myself in the webcam, even record myself.

A few times I would sloppily take off my makeup on purpose in order to be "caught" and have to explain myself. We had a discussion specifically about me not leaving the apartment in her clothes and how that would make us both uncomfortable. I was desperately in love and trying to make it in a new city. Maintaining the relationship so I had a place to live, not to mention the other supports that come along with being in a (presumed) cishet relationship became my priority for years. Universal basic income would have solved a lot of these issues for me.

I did a Bigger Coming Out in 2013, like "you need to know how serious this is." At the end of my rope, I didn't even care about breaking up by that point. I came out to my therapist, a close friend, and started dressing up at home openly. The first time she saw me in makeup we both laughed. Soon after I started doing what I called "lady walks" or "confidence walks" by going outside en femme. I bought a wig, learned how to shop for clothes in public with only minor panic, and went full throttle into YouTube makeup tutorials. I devoted so many hours to just painting on one look over and over again like I was but resisted harder than ever. That's not to say it couldn't have been done properly, in a kink way, it just didn't happen like that for me. Forced femme stories, though, are fantasy. They usually ended on a happy note, or never ended at all. "Part 3 coming soon!" lingering on a post from 2003, the conclusion hanging in the air for all time, teasing hope. Good fantasy fulfills a desire or explores feelings that are too challenging (or boring) to direct head on. Wanna explore oppressive political systems through the haunting lens of childhood innocence? Cool, here's *Lord of the Flies*. Wanna explore your unrelenting desire to be a woman but feel so fucked up about what the world would do to you? Forced femme stories.

I moved to Ontario at 18 so I could live in an apartment with my girlfriend at the time, who I came out to as having worn her clothes and makeup pretty much once a year between 18 and 23. I had a hard time finding a job (something to do with anxiety and the will to live???). She would leave for work or school and I would be in a locked apartment by myself for hours at a time, days in a row. With all of her clothes. And makeup. And this halloween wig I had with cute lil' devil horns. It was the first time I could dress up regularly.

I had bigger feet than her, but there was this one pair of wrap up heels that I was able to fit into. I would work a radioactive knot in my stomach loosen. One story in particular has a mother dress her presumed son in girl clothes, I forget for what reason, and parade them around during her daily activities. Introducing them to the neighbours as her daughter. Buying girl clothes at the department store. The child is unsure, scared, resistant at first, but ultimately the trust between the two leads to the child expressing the desire for being a girl from now on. It is tender and loving in a way that a trans girl would know as supportive, though others may see as abusive.

I am writing this in a public place and am nearly in tears recalling it because it so powerfully describes what I wish could have happened for me. The mental gymnastics we force trans kids to go through is utter brutality. Spending your life shifting between "girlmode" and "boymode" is like staring at clouds trying to discern what shapes you see in them every second of your life. Do I see a girl? Do I see a boy? Everyone sees a boy. I often mistake wishing I'd been born cis when I really just wish I'd been identified as a trans girl from infancy. My body isn't an inherent problem but a learned one. "Frozen needs" are a classic therapist term for unmet desires we carry with us into adulthood. Petticoat punishment stories put me into a safe little submarine and take me into the depths of my frozen needs to show me what an ideal trans girlhood might've looked like.

Now, I've actually been force femmed without consent a couple times in my life. IT IS BAD. It wasn't like in the stories. I didn't suddenly give in to my womanly desires,

The classics I gravitated towards had a lot to do with lack of consent stuff. A bunch of tough femmes or hulking men take it upon themselves to sissify the main character for their own ends, usually for sex and/or labour. They always have "plans" for you which I found immensely cathartic (gosh yes someone else tell me what to do, please!!). The plots change, but the feeling stays the same: we must force you because you're too weak to do it yourself. So the person goes through some trial of being kept in a cage and forcibly given hormones or locked in ridiculously tall heels, makeup forcibly applied, and need to serve drinks to (or get on your knees and blow) a mansion full of guests as your newly girl self. Stephen has become Stephanie. She squeaks out her best female voice and is mocked for it, punished for her failure, but given "lessons" how to do it better. Sometimes the goal is pure humiliation, but other stories end with the character accepting themselves and becoming a confident woman in their own right by the end. Your tormentors believe in you.

Petticoat punishment is a subgenre that, from what I've seen, leans less on humiliation and sex, and more towards the physical and emotional transformation from boy to girl. The power dynamic is more child-adult, and the punishments are "I will force you to dress like a girl as punishment for being a rotten child", but can also take the form of, "I am doing this to you because I wish it, you have no choice, but I am also wondering, would you like to dress like this all the time? You want to be a pretty girl, don't you? I can tell." Fuuuuuuuuuuuuuuuuuuuuuck did those stories hit me. Even as I write this I can feel

This was a common narrative. People who really liked dressing like girls but were totally not into transitioning. Drag queens? Check. Sissies? Check! Transvestites? Check! Internet crossdressers? Double check. We had so much in common! That final phrase, "but I'm not transitioning." So I thought, huh! Me neither! Rumour has it she left the web to transition privately with her wife and child, but I don't know for sure, and that's ok! (but am dyinggggg to know).

When I look back, I knew what I wanted, but everyone around me, even those most like me, were telling me: Don't do it. Today, my gender is like whatever the fuck. I'm a girl. I deal with bullshit cissexist standards of how I should live my life and I wake up everyday figuring out how to navigate it that day. But I made multiple decisions throughout my childhood, teen years, and early adulthood that my wanting to be a girl must never be given into, despite having started researching hormones seriously at 17.

This is also around the same time I started going hard into forced femme stories, sometimes called forced feminization, sissification, or petticoat punishment. I found a lot of these stories on literotica.com, written by folks who were passionate amateur writers of the subject. Forced femme is a type of erotica that puts male-assigned people in situations where they are forcibly made to dress in feminine clothing or to act in feminine ways. *Mrs.Doubtfire* is NOT an example of forced feminization because it is about a man who had lots of options and lied to his family out of complete selfishness. Forced femme stories are about putting femininity forward as a real option one could pursue, and in fact, must.

I look back on IDing this way as part of my burgeoning, unstoppable womanhood. Ultimately, crossdresser was just a placeholder. But it was something I had to grapple with before being able to move forward. Some might see the fact that I knew I wanted to be a girl at such a young age as a privileged position, but I don't see how that's possible. Having that knowledge from such a young age let me build powerful, internal logic systems to punish myself for desiring a girlhood for 2 decades. Without help, the Knowing was useless. By the mid 2000's, the Internet was finally becoming the kind of help I needed. Let's go over some of the resources I came across.

First and foremost, we have Aubrey Frost, my guardian angel. I count her as one of the key people in the world who saved my life. I don't know her because, as so often with girls like us, she's from the Internet! Aubrey's Place was a simple early 2000's website where she hosted her own selfies and photoshoots accompanied with some updates about her life now and then. I lived for these updates. You can still see some of it today. The Internet Archive shows her website like this:

"Welcome to Aubrey's Place! Here you'll get a chance to get to know all about me, a 23 y.o. part-time T-girl from Michigan. I've been doing this whole T-thing since I was about 13. For a time, it seemed that I may want to transition. But, that time has passed, and now I realize that I don't feel strongly enough about it to take it any further. So I'm having fun with it, and nothing more. I do not live as a girl, nor do I ever plan to."

The Early 2000's

I used to be ashamed about people seeing me identify as a crossdresser. It's the term I first used with my friends and parents. I felt shame that I couldn't admit to myself what I wanted because decades of internalized transmisogyny and the overt threat of violence made me feel like I wasn't trans and definitely wasn't a woman.

That's due in no small part to the individual-centric model of our shitty neoliberal, society. It affects people in the closet by forcing us to be the ones who individually enact "coming out", while everyone else is positioned as being the ones who deal with it, their shock and reactions justified, the comfortable feeling of "ah, this person didn't come out because it was their own problem in a vacuum and I didn't contribute to it whatsoever!"---> AS OPPOSED TO a true community that prepares at all times for the infinite ways we can support each other, which is often confused with pseudo-supportive sentiments like "we always knew" and "we don't care" and "we were waiting for *you* to figure it out" which frames pacificity and active silence as a form of legitimate support, BUT ANYWAYYYYYYYY

breathes

woman. I've somehow become a spokesperson for gender non-comformity in general. I work at a library and there are few instances of someone pulling me aside to tell me about an amazing book about a trans girl. 95% of the time I am excitedly shown books on boys wearing dresses with stories about overcoming bullying. I've yet to come across a children's book about a gender nonconforming AMAB child who goes on a fun adventure with dragons and magic. The selling point is always, this boy is wearing a dress and everyone is kind and open-minded enough to support him after he does an immense amount of work to convince everyone to enact basic decency towards a child!

It's bittersweet that people think of me when they see these books cuz I'm not a boy in a dress, and even if I had been supported to ID as such when I was younger, saying "I'm a girl, actually" wouldn't have gone over well. So when I wear my makeup and my clothes, no matter what, I'm a fucking femme and always have been. Even if I called it crossdressing. Even when I'm referred to as "young man" in my winged eyeliner and pencil skirt. I can't force you to see me as a woman, but I leave no room for wondering if I'm a femme. You can misgender me in a skirt but the fact I'm in a skirt means I fucking win.

how to feel sexy, how to feel kinky, years before I started masturbating. It always had to do with the nebulous "oh my god" feeling of being a good girl. At one point, I had straight up stolen a bra, pantyhose, sweater, and skirt from my mother and locked them in this IKEA cupboard I had. To make up for not being able to wear those clothes during the day, to not be able to feel "tired" in them, to feel like I wore them so long I wanted to take them off, I would sleep in those clothes. I would sleep in heels when I could sneak it.

One of the goofier ways I got misgendered last year was when I held a door open for a coworker and he said, "Thank you sir… or ma'am! You're wearing pants today so I can't tell". I didn't necessarily see pants as a femme artifact, but I'm starting to out of spite. And power tools and electric guitars and hiking boots and, fuck it, grey colour schemes for living rooms. Beef jerky is femme now. In fact, iT'S ALWAYS BEEN FEMME. WHATCHA GONNA DO NOW, GENDERS?

Let's be fair. Makeup and clothes aren't under the ownership of womanhood. Obviously, anyone can wear makeup and dresses. But it's soooooooooo frustrating the way people are more likely to say "boys can wear dresses" and not "trans girls can wear dresses". There's no room made for people who had outwardly identified as men in makeup and dresses to actually be women. That jump is apparently too far. I'll get misgendered for the rest of my life. Certain people just see me as a man in a dress and that is less offensive to them than just accepting me as a remember as a kid before a social event she was applying some to herself in the bathroom and I could not stop bugging her and flitting around, being shooed away until it dried. I just wanted to be around that smell. Nail polish, to me, required some sort of WHIMIS training, as nail polish remover smelled like acid and I didn't know if we even had any. Being in the business of hiding my feminine desires, nail polish was too permanent, so I admired it from afar until I was in my 20's. When I was first exploring coming out more seriously in 2013, I wore nail polish on my toes. I was working a warehouse job at the time and would take off steel toed boots in the bathroom to dissuade the mounting dysphoria, admiring my bright and tired feet. Nowadays, I'm always wearing nail polish as it provides a constant relief and reminder of who I am. Going without it for even a day is a bad feeling.

Clothing was its own category of fun and misery. It opens up a lot of questions about why wearing skirts and dresses made me feel like a girl (have fun arguing about that with TERFS). I counterbalanced not being able to wear fun femme clothing by wearing, like, funny t-shirts? Wearing my mother's dresses and skirts were this insatiable, tortured desire. As a preteen I was already practicing how to unclasp a bra, one-handed behind my back. Wire bras. Push up bras. Wanting boobs, a common thing a young girl would want. Pantyhose was so coooooooool. I love pantyhose today, too. It's light and feels cool on your body. I liked how it shaped my crotch. I liked how delicate it was, how soft I had to be with it or it'd break and I'd be caught. Black pantyhose just made me feel sexy. I learned preferred the ease of something like blush, which I applied to my cheeks like a dainty little elf. Or, I packed it on like mortar because the MORE BLUSH the MORE I AM GIRL!

Hair was the physical embodiment of cutting my gender out of my body. My hair is curly, like, 3a/3b if you want to go with the hair scale developed by Oprah's lifelong hair stylist (I'm serious). Even at a few inches long it would begin to curl, especially at the back of my neck. I had my hair cut often as a kid, shutting my eyes closed and needing my mother to stand literally RIGHT BESIDE ME while it was happening, feeling so heartsick and traumatized as the parts that scared me so much softly floated to the barber's floor, only to dutifully grow back. "Curls are for girls!" I would yell at adults everytime it was suggested my hair was "gorgeous" or "beautiful" or "like a girls" or "wasted on a boy". How many times did I want to give in and let them know HI YES I AM A GIRL THANK YOU FOR NOTICING PLEASE SAVE ME I AM GOLDILOCKS. I gave myself as fully over to my assigned gender as possible lest I experience the consequences of vocalizing how much femininity is actually cool in a society that absolutely fucking hates femininity, especially on people born with a dick. Oh well. Today my curly pink/purple/red/blonde hair bounces just at my shoulders and I've even learned to cut it myself!

Nail polish is a throbbing-deep-in-my-chest femme artifact. It was one of the few products my mother regularly used, and I loved seeing it being done. I was made with just me in mind. I loved acting out scenes from movies and TV shows where women and girls would play around with makeup. I remember my grandma telling me "it's a shame you're a boy, you have such beautiful eyelashes!" I was nicknamed "Tweety Bird" as a baby. The bigger issue with me wearing makeup as a kid was that zero evidence could be left behind. Lipstick was pretty straight forward. If my lips were too red well, fuckin', I ate some candy. But mascara is the most obvious and the most difficult to remove without melting your own eyes. So I would only experiment with the goopy fluff stick when I knew I also had time to remove it afterwards, which involved hot water, soap, a cloth, and pain. Femme is pain and I earned my stripes mother fuckers.

Eye shadow was weird. The line between "I feel like a girl" and "raccoon face paint" was slim, and I didn't have the dexterity or knowhow to pull it off. I often put eye shadow to the side, or used it sparingly and disappointingly. Today, I battle dysphoria stemming from my face, my brow, of my semi-hooded eyes, but with the knowledge that the beautiful application of eye shadow I pull off daily on such features is mastery of the form (did you doubt I was a Capricorn for even a second).

Eyeliner I don't remember touching the stuff. I'm a liquid eyeliner wizard now, but back then the concept was totally alien. I remember a girl in grade 4 was sent home to take off her eyeliner and I was so confused about A) why the fuck it was a problem in the first place and B) what the fuck eyeliner even was. Stuff was too hard to use, I

During the start of my transition I began the painful and ongoing process of centering my femmeness as the default setting as opposed to something I "learn" or "am taught" from the cis world around me. Exploring my femmeness put certain artifacts above others in terms of interest and meaning. Allow me to go over some of them.

Lipstick was and is so serious to me. Used to give me so many butterflies in the tummy. It was the most easily identifiable makeup I could quickly grab from my mother's bathroom drawer, and I even knew how to apply it! "Lipstick" just sounds naughty. I would kiss myself in the mirror and make lip shapes all over it. I love the sickly perfumey smell, and rotating a tube to reveal a ruby cylinder to apply on myself brings me all the way back in time. For me, wearing lipstick isn't just an act of resistance or a feminine expression, it's a reconnecting with my young, damaged femme self. I get to connect with a fucked up little girl and without words I get to tell her "we wear as much fucking lipstick as we want." I recall watching an episode of *Buffy* with my family where Xander is force femmed with makeup and clothes as part of a fraternity (which gave me enough sissy feelings for a lifetime). Later in the episode, Angel looks at Xander and asks, "Are you wearing… lipstick?" and I could have melted in my seat right then and there. Why yes Angel, you ageless creep, I *am* wearing lipstick.

Mascara was another simple to use piece of makeup, along with the eyelash curler. I have these long, wavy lashes and this was the only piece of makeup I really felt

Femme is Crossdressing is Femme is...

masculinity was their artifice/rip it away/
femininity/always the heart of us/trans girls be free.
- G.L.O.S.S., "Masculine Artifice"

Coming into my own femmeness and identifying as femme has been a whole 'nother dimension to my transition. Coming to the understanding that I have always been femme and have been expressing myself as such since I was a child is a concept my heart barely lets me feel. It's hard to purge the idea that since I presented as masc or boylike most of my life, that meant I wasn't femme. And if you're feeling that way too, I want you to know it's total bullshit. Femme has as much to do with attitude as it does aesthetic. I had to peek at my femmeness in a mirror, alone and scared. It means quickly stuffing a hair clip I found on the ground into my pocket to try on later. It means training my ears to perk up when even the slightest floorboard creak could indicate someone was about walk in on me dressing up. It means learning how to steal.

As the night wore on, guy friends put on the nail polish and makeup in a joyous celebration of their cis confidence. "We'll put some on you!" Nope. Ugh. I hated this. I burn through the evening in total damage control, turning down every attempt to be force femmed in that space, with those people, further cementing in my heart the knowledge that performing femininity in front of others would kill me, since that's all I ever saw happen to girls like me.

Precious Mems

About 14 years old. Attending the local cross country ski club banquet. I hear there's a competition this year for a prize. The competition is for the most colourfully dressed at the event. Oh, I can do that! I can do Hawaiian shirts. I win! The room is packed with people. I receive the prize in a fun gift bag! Standing tall on a table like a gold medal podium recipient I open it. What's in it?

My whole body stiffens standing over the banquet attendees, triumphant cries of "what's in the bag?!" echo from wall to wall. I can't say the words. It's too hard. I grab a few items from inside the bag and hold it out for everyone to see. It's nail polish and makeup. The organizers of the competition naturally assumed the "most colourfully dressed" would be a girl. I look at my mother who mouths "oh noo", the kind of "oh no" that could only cut a closeted sissy in half, as if to say, "oh no, he hates girl stuff". The kind of "oh no" that can only be harvested from a history of telling everyone how much I do hate girl stuff, how much I hate being compared to a girl, the distance I was forced to put there for harmful reasons, and seeing that work reflected back at me in that moment with people who were stronger and better than me at a sport that would have vilified me if I'd come out as trans.

body splintered into infinite versions, with each corridor becoming impossibly dark forever into the void. I could see myself looking at myself a million times over.

Although there was a full length mirror in the bedroom that I regularly admired myself in, I would often sneak heels into the bathroom so I could lock the door for extra security. My absolute favourites were a pair of red pumps with ankle straps. Wearing those were my first feeling of being sexy. Standing on the toilet lid so I could see my feet in the mirror and admire my strapped up feet. I would lay towels down on the floor to muffle the sounds of my strutting and pose for myself. And just so I could feel like a tripped-out space alien, I would turn on the red heat lamp and crouch in the sink, pulling the mirrors closed around me. An infinite number of me in ankle strap pumps, bathed in heat and redness. It was like astral projection and that was some of the moments I felt closest to being celestial. Not long after, the shoes no longer fit.

image in the mirror was and still is vital to my heart. There are those brief moments, squinting my eyes where I could convince myself there was a girl.

I recall in early December, I believed I was the only one home, save a brother downstairs. I'd checked the driveway AND the office! Shirtless with a shower running down the hall, I was raiding my parent's closet. Anything would do. Just to make my heart feel the way I wanted. Just to see that self image reflected back for a minute.

My father walks into the room. This is the first and only time I'd been caught red-handed. Without missing a beat I recite my pre-planned excuse, "I was looking for presents!" and ran out. We were nearing Christmas, after all. That is a one-time excuse and is valid only three weeks of the year. Heart racing, I shut the bathroom door behind me. The shower's steam filled the room. That could never happen again. The mirror fogged up.

Raiding my parent's closet also involved sneaking into the en-suite bathroom. So much shit in there to be mesmerized by. Flower smelling powders, makeup, shaving tools, a red toned heat lamp installed above the soaker tub, removable plastic Spock ears for some reason. The most noteworthy feature, though, has to be the triple mirror medicine cabinet. All facing the same direction, with the two outside mirrors at a slight angle inwards and on hinges. I was small enough to be able to crouch in the sink and close the mirrors fully around me. I was instantly transported to this omni-dimensional bizarro-world. My the open, I would do it in private (hint: this is where the seeds of trauma are planted). Once I was old enough to be left home alone, wearing my mother's clothes increased in frequency. Sometimes I would just touch it all, finger through the rack of clothes, compare a heel to the size of my own foot for future use, maybe even sneak it on real quick and run back to my room, filled with exhilaration. Other times I would sit in my room having a near panic attack, psyching myself up just to cross my legs, hang my wrist, or pout my lips.

I remember I would grab her clothes and dress up IN THE SHOWER. Let me explain. Having the shower on gave me a good 30-minute timeline alone and I could hide everything in a towel afterwards and sneak the clothes into the laundry room later. There was this itchy, acrylic, baby blue sweater in particular that I loved to wear, along with any pencil style skirt I could find. Steamy water spread all over me, the soaking wet fabric slowly sagging and enveloping my body in its warm compression. A few moments in and the sweater looked like it was melting off my body. The neck hole almost became so large it could fall off my shoulders. I'd let it happen. The sweater would hit the shower floor with a loud *SLOP*. I would come to my senses when the water pelted loudly off the skirt like rain on a tarp, convincing me that anyone hearing this nearby would come to the exact conclusion of my embarrassing deed.

As sensational as this experience was, solitary access to the mirror was still the most important part. Confirming my

I remember the feeling of flying around the department store's girl section trying on anything I desired. There was no fear of reprisal in those brief moments. It felt like getting into a hot shower after coming in from a cold winter outside. My numb extremities would feel a rush of heat and get tingly numb.

So, imagine if you will the glacier cold shock of waking up. And the longstanding disappointment every night when I wouldn't be able to dream it. Instead, I would have run of the mill shit: teeth falling out, spiders in my bed. Sometimes ~*~kissing dreams~*~ or hand holding.

Here's what conjuring my dreams would look like. I would lie in my bed and with my eyes shut and covers over my head. It's the closest I could get to pure isolation. I imagined what I wanted. Like in the movie *I Am Legend*, except Will Smith keeps stealing dresses from abandoned department stores instead of verbally abusing mannequins. As I grew older, the dream wasn't enough. It was a nice memory, but I couldn't control it, and waiting months at a time was painful.

I remember being put in my mother's clothes at a very young age, with these clip on earrings and dancing around for my family, who laughed along with me. But after a few minutes there was a clear, ok enough of that. Everything was put away and all I remember is the vague understanding of, oh, I'm not allowed to do that. Yet, that's all I ever wanted to do. The expression in that aesthetic was the purest essence of myself, and if I couldn't do it in

Does the Mirror World Go on Forever?

Six years old/Staring at my nose in the mirror/
Trying to dip my toes in the mirror/
Thinking 'Who's that girl?'/
And 'Does the mirror world go on forever?'
- Lianne La Havas, "Green and Gold"

I started to wish that I was a girl from around 4 or 5. Blowing out my birthday candles: "I wish I was a girl". That's just how it went. Sometimes I wish I'd win the lottery. But in my mind that was only for the means of turning into a girl. Buying the machine that I imagined in my dreams. Once every few months I would have it. The Big Dream.

It would usually take place in a department store after closing. That was the most important part. No one else was around. Most times there would be a big square machine with an opening on both sides. A conveyor belt ran along the floor from one end to the other. I would gleefully step onto the conveyor belt, enter the machine one end and exit the other end totally transformed. Imagine Goldilocks: blonde, curly hair, frilly pink dress, white tights, and shiny black mary janes on my feet. A tidy princess.

Hold your gender up to a microscope, not necessarily because you might in fact be a different gender than the one assigned at birth (but you might be, ha ha!) but also because there is some toxic shit you have absolutely internalized about your gender that you might not want to keep anymore. I haven't just hacked and slashed my way into wondering what kind of person I want to be, but what kind of woman I want to be. If you've put no effort into examining what your gender means to you, I'd recommend grabbing a blanket, a fizzy drink, putting on "Graduation Song" by Vitamin C, and doing a ponder on the subject.

What are you looking forward to post-transition?
Being a content and happy person that actually wants to go outside and do stuff. Not be so fucking depressed.

I was 25 and it was the first time anyone had ever asked me flat out what gender I wanted to be. I had never been encouraged to take time to think about it and write it down. These questions were life saving. They're the type of questions that should be mandatory for everyone. Not just what gender do you want to be, but what kind of person do you want to be and how does your gender function within that.

Here's a journal excerpt from September 15, 2015. I was to be waitlisted for hormones for over a full year and was desperate to know myself:

What is your gender goal here?
I want desperately to look like a girl.

Do you identify as a girl?
I don't know what that means

What does looking like a girl mean to you?
Smooth, soft skin, boobs, cutie face, cutie hair, doing everything she wants in life, owning at life so hard
She's fit and charming and so fucking fashionable and somehow talented in multiple disciplines. She's smart and hardworking and very loving. She's a goddamn professional. She's an outdoors enthusiast. She's a feminist and loves women. Like, a lot. When she goes to shows, as she does often, she looks so good.

Who do you think or hope you will be on the other side of this?
I want boobs, hips, butt, smooth skin and a feminine voice. I want a girl singing voice. I want to pass. I want to feel comfortable with myself. I want to get on with my life and hobbies already!

What are your worries and fears?
- Loss of partner
- Loss of job/potential career
- Harassment and violence
- Not passing
- Not believing in myself
- Being gross and undesirable
- Having to deal with my family
- Not being able to travel internationally
- Transition regret
- Lack of results
- Shit voice

What are your hopes and dreams?
- Being deliriously happy
- Pursuing my fucking hobbies and passions as myself
- Just effortless being
- A lifelong weight off my shoulders
- Passing
- Referred to as a girl but also engaging with genderfluidity
- Boobs, soft skin
- NO HAIR ON MY FACE

The Guide

In 2014 I found a transition ebook called "Hacking Transition". The woman who wrote it sold it to other trans women and those questioning in order to fund her bottom surgery. The document details every step in transition one would need instructions on, from helping answer "am I trans?" to laser hair removal, to surgery, to clothes, to voice lessons. This document is a prime example of the type of information you can access on the Internet that changed my life. A workbook section at the beginning of the guide asks the confused gender nerd how to come to conclusions about themselves. Below are the questions and answers I hand-wrote in a journal back in 2014, with no corrections, and are a great example of the anguish and uncertainty I felt at the time:

How do you currently identify?
Transgender and genderfluid. I generally feel genderless, but I just know I want to look like a girl a lot.

How do you think this might change?
I don't think it'll change my identity, but I could see identifying as a girl more strongly.

look sad, weak, or broken. These phrases became a quiet rallying cry for me, and at the same time it condemned me to a similar future of embarrassment and shame if I didn't keep things under wraps.

One of the earliest oases for internet trans information was Susan's Place, which exists today. It was pretty much the only trans website of its kind you could find in the 90's, or at least the most popular for a while. It was forum based, and mostly adults posted there, IDing as trans, transsexuals, transvestites, sissies, crossdressers, etc. I was a child. My life on the Internet, at its peak, was MSN Messenger and flash games. No tumblr. No trans YouTube stars. No Jazz Jennings. No *Nevada*. Susan's Place wasn't really meant for me. I knew of it, and may have even visited it back then. But these things were, I thought, secret crossdresser shit and something I couldn't research as the family computer resided openly in the kitchen. Any information I was able to find merely fueled the concept that it was necessary to hide these things from everyone I knew. Well, it worked! (insert crying emoji here). So, crossdresser it was for me. Literally, what other option did I have?

Wanting to die is a pretty common thing I've heard from trans people. Understanding my trans self at a young age meant imagining myself wanting to be reborn. I'd often daydream about reaching the end of my life and going to a Service Ontario style Heaven kiosk with lineups and different menus of things I could order. In this foggy, bright lighted waiting area I would finally be able to check in with the angel-winged clerks and let them know, "Ya that was wrong, I wanna be a girl this time." I wasn't even ten years old and I was deciding that my life wasn't good enough to bother with.

90's cable TV also included Dame Edna at *Just For Laughs* and RuPaul way back when. While drag queens were the most accepted form of gender nonconformity in 90's pop culture, it was made abundantly clear at the time that they were men. Episodes of *KinK* would play on Showtime around midnight and I'd sneak out of my room to catch a glimpse of fetish gear and gender play. Shit like *Jerry Springer* would come on and someone would use the phrase "born in the wrong body" or "woman in a man's body".

That became my MANTRA. I was like OHHHH. I was born in the wrong BODY, I see! That became my life for a long time, despite it not being accurate. I'd keep an ear out, radaring for any slip of the phrase "born in the wrong body" as it felt more accurate. It was also made clear to me that other people besides myself were CLEARLY suffering from this. But as it was, they were adults. So all I ever saw were adults being probed and questioned and made to

None of these pieces were overtly Capital-T Trans per se. And what that does to a young mind is reinforce the idea that it's just dressing, just for jokes. The Lumberjack is mocked by those around him who repeat with confusion, "He puts on women's clothing? And hangs around in bars?". *Cybersix* is simply using a clever alias. In one episode, Steve Carey responds to a bartender refusing to serve him cheap drinks at Ladies' Night prices, "I may not be a woman, but I am a lady!" This line stuck with me as much as it confused me.

Jadzia Dax on *Star Trek: Deep Space Nine* is probably the closest thing to capital-T Trans representation I had growing up. Dax's race, the trill, can bond with symbionts, which are these small, gooey, ice cream cone shaped aliens that transfer from trill to trill as each host dies, creating a chain of near-infinite lifetimes from host to host. The signature makeup for the trill are these cute leopard-like spots on their bodies. I have freckles and often imagined myself as Dax. She would refer to her past self like "back when I was a father/husband" or "I've been a man before". On occasion she would introduce herself as Jadzia, but say, "You might remember me as Curzon". Friends from her past might refer to her as "Curzon", or even just "old man". This drop dead gorgeous woman with the cutest leopard markings on her body is being lovingly called "old man" on 90's cable television and everyone was ok with it and it was endearing?! You best believe I daydreamed about getting a new host. That my symbiont would be transferred to a girl when I died.

it palatable for mainstream audiences. The "gotcha" scene where his kid finds him peeing standing up, well, that sucks and is played for "women don't have bodies like that!!!" laughs.

Really, though, the whole "lying to my family and disrespecting the rights of my ex-wife who, in hindsight, seems completely justified in her misgivings about letting our children spend time with me" thing seems like a pretty huge slap in the face of, you know, MEN? Considering the character is a man? The way the film makes a hero from this type of behaviour in men as a gag is much more alarming to me than the lazy transmisogyny. Like, a cis man pretending to be a cis woman to trick his family IS outrageous. It's quite bad! Perhaps the biggest gag of all is that dudes who are really into analyzing the exploitation of men in media don't seem as invested in deconstructing the conclusions made in *Mrs.Doubtfire* the way trans people do. This film makes ya look like shit, my dudes!

Here's some more 90s media that gave me weird feelings: Monty Python's "Lumberjack Song" is about a burly lumberjack who "puts on women's clothing and hangs around in bars". *Cybersix* was an animated series depicting a femme superheroine who wore a black, skin tight leather bodysuit at night and masqueraded as a dude professor during the day. Drew's brother, Steve, on the *Drew Carey Show* is a self-proclaimed crossdresser. One episode has him attending a baseball game in boy-mode, to Drew's request, before Steve pulls his pants down to reveal fluffy panties underneath as he laughs at his brother's embarrassment.

I was in the complete fucking dark. What ends up happening is that these movies and all this media? THAT becomes your community. That's your way into discovering what else is out there. Identifying as a trans woman becomes synonymous with hating trans women.

There's another level at which this stings, which is I can't enjoy a comedy about, and let me put this in bold so you really feel it, a **PET DETECTIVE**. That premise is SO funny. And I can't enjoy it! The main plot was about the theft of a football team's live dolphin. Like. It's wacky, it's silly, it's slapstick. There's Star Trek impressions. It didn't need to be transmisogyny incarnate. But it was. So part of me still likes it, because fuck, the idea of a **PET DETECTIVE** is still stuck in my mind two decades later and I can't stop thinking about how funny this premise is. There was a penguin living in his freezer for fuck's sake! But also, trannies are villainous. And wearing a tutu is a costume you put on when you're trying to "act crazy" and sneak into a psych ward to find clues. Why did they ruin their good ideas with bad ideas? Just have a fun pet caper!

Mrs. Doubtfire was another mega hit of the 90's, but I don't inherently hate the premise for its transmisogyny per se. Let me explain. The scene where he says "make me a woman" and gets made up in different lady outfits was REALLY IMPORTANT TO ME AS A CLOSETED TRANS KID. A superstar comedian in a role where he actively WANTS to be feminized, even as a laugh, was better representation than anything else I'd seen. The fact that it was played for laughs is, unfortunately, what made

A major component of growing up trans without modern Internet is the violently transphobic media, TV shows, and movies. Allow me to go over a few of the more important ones (also, Buzzfeed wrote "25 Years of Transphobia in Comedy" go read that, too).

I was six when *Ace Ventura* came out. The big twist in this detective plot is that the chief of police in the investigation is in fact the perpetrator of the crime. Ace, played by Jim Carrey, could not comprehend the evidence in front of him suggesting the mysteriously vanished football player Ray Finkle is actually *gasp!* police chief Lois Einhorn! Ace, who was kissed by Einhorn earlier in the movie, spits, burns his clothes, and cries in the shower upon this discovery, every shot played for comedy. At the end he unveils *THE TRUTH* by tearing off Einhorn's clothes and revealing a CLOSE UP of her tucked genitals bulging between her legs and underwear to the physical revulsion of the police officers surrounding her.

What the hell, Jim???

Watching stuff like this, the adults around me, the entire world around me, TOLD me, with their actions, their laughs, the money they spent at the box office, the reruns casually playing on TV in almost every room in the house, that laughing at trans women in movies was good. That women with beautiful, gorgeous bulges were disgusting and treacherous and actually secretly men. And no community, as far as I could tell, that felt this wasn't a fine thing to believe.

Being Trans in the 90's and, Good Lord, the Media

The 90's were so cool, right?! We had Aqua and *Fifth Element* and the Spice Girls. Pizza Huts were super popular. McDonald's had fun hamburger chairs. Orbitz was a weird phase, admittedly, but we got past that. We got past that.

The 90's were also a tedious and interminable stretch of lifeless desert for a trans kid. Technology to counteract oppressive institutions and mindsets improved unhurriedly. I'm thinking of a specific type of technology here.

I'm talking about the Internet.

But, I'm not talking about the Internet as it stands now, or even as it stood ten years ago. 3G? Wireless? What? I mean 90's Internet. Dial-up. I was born in 1988, so the Internet of the 90's didn't mean anything to me. If you're a Gen X'er and did a hack or wrote code or installed Mosaic or did some deep web shit to take part in chat rooms, I don't know about that.

Introduction

I identified as a crossdresser until 2014. My therapist at the time mentioned a queer camp in my area that I might consider volunteering with. This would be a big first step for me coming out. Filling out the application I was bowled over by some of the questions like, "What does anti-oppression mean to you?" and "Do you have ASIST training?" I was like, shit, I don't know!

They also asked, "How do you identify?"

My answer: I identify as a recently out gender-fluid person with bicurious tendencies from Scottish and Ukrainian ancestry (white crossdresser works too!).

This zine is a collection of thoughts, stories, and excerpts from my journal. I reflect back on my time growing up as a closeted trans kid in the 90's and 2000's. This isn't a history of crossdressing. It's about my history and how crossdressing fits into it.

My name is Kat Rogue. I am a white she/her dykefag trans girl. This zine was written while on unceded Algonquin territory.

Content warnings: dysphoria, childhood memories, depression, mentions of suicide/wanting to die, transphobic media, erotic details about, like, ME.

This zine is dedicated to
all the girls who didn't know they could.

Crossdresser: Growing Up Trans in the 1990s and 2000s
Kat Rogue

Sheer Spite Press
www.sheerspitepress.ca

Design and layout by Lee Pepper for Sheer Spite Press.

Library and Archives Canada
ISBN 978-1-7753304-1-7

CROSS-DRESSER

GROWING UP TRANS IN THE 1990s AND 2000s

KAT ROGUE